Seven Steps to
FREEDOM

DARRELL MOWAT

WESTBOW®
PRESS
A DIVISION OF THOMAS NELSON
& ZONDERVAN

WestBow Press books may be ordered through booksellers or by contacting:

WestBow Press
A Division of Thomas Nelson & Zondervan
1663 Liberty Drive
Bloomington, IN 47403
www.westbowpress.com
1 (866) 928-1240

ISBN: 978-1-4908-3321-7 (sc)
ISBN: 978-1-4908-3322-4 (e)

Library of Congress Control Number: 2014906609

Printed in the United States of America.

WestBow Press rev. date: 08/07/2014

Contents

Acknowledgements

To everyone who made this Bible study possible thank you and to God be the glory!

Seven Steps to Freedom is dedicated to everyone who is in captivity right now. Keep up the good fight. There is a light at the end of the tunnel.

Before starting this study keep an open mind and if you have a higher power ask for wisdom and understanding for this book to enter your heart.

Introduction

I never thought I would see the inside of a jail cell. As a child I always thought if I started smoking I would get involved with a gang and start stealing, so I did my best to stay away from that stuff.

But God has a funny way of working out a person's preconceived notions of others, even as a child. As He says, "Judge not, and you will not be judged" (Luke 6:37). So after eight years of a relatively blissful life as a child my mother and father had a divorce. With my life situation abruptly changed it was now time for the next phase of my life.

It was not always easy growing up in a single parent home. Thank God my mom and dad did the best they could when I was young to prepare me for life. My dad taught me the basics in using tools and encouraged scouting activities as a young child. And my mom took me to community activities for reading, sports and play time with other children.

As I grew older I started swaying from my upbringing. I hung-out with neighbourhood friends and school mates where, at times, we caused some minor trouble and mischief. I was bullied and abused by some of these people and I had done the same to others. But in the end we did enjoy ourselves, as well, learning how to play our schoolyard games and get along in the world.

As I moved on and high school was right around the corner, I was entering a new world of responsibility. College or work was just five years away and either one required focus in order to succeed. Again, unfortunately I chose a more reckless path for a time. I enjoyed high school life, as I had a good educational foundation from elementary school. I started working part-time on the weekends during school and fulltime during the summer. With the money, instead of saving it for college, I drank it away on the weekends, bought a car and invested in loud car stereo equipment.

I thought this was all grand until my drinking got out of control and I lost my vehicle and almost lost my life.

After this wakeup call, I decided it was time to "pull up my socks" and do the right thing. This meant focusing on a University career path.

University was a culture-shock at first, big buildings, more students and an incredible infrastructure, not to mention the diversity of nationalities of the student and faculty groups. It was a great and refreshing change in my life and I embraced it.

I can remember the first class I sat in. I said to myself "Wow, I cannot believe I am here". Being in awe for a few minutes, I finally realized, "Well I better start listening and studying or I will not be here for very long". So that was the start of my University career.

It took four years to complete the studies required to meet my degree choice. And I enjoyed every minute of it. I met new people, learned new things about myself, the world and had the chance to travel while doing it. Namely, I was part of a team that designed, constructed, and raced a canoe of concrete. This was the start of learning how to lead a group of people to a common goal.

In my final year of University I realized I had some decisions to make. I had a small fortune in debt and the desire to accomplish more. I was not ready for the "working world" and I found an option of joining the military would be an opportune choice at the time. This worked because they had a signing bonus for engineers, which was my discipline and the possibility to become a pilot, as I had dreamed about being one over the years past.

With that path as a good option and graduation right around the corner, I "got serious" and started the application process. During this time before I joined there were a few bumps in the road. That is, my Grandfather passed away and my mother had cancer, but nevertheless it was time to move onto the next chapter of my life.

In advance of starting my military training I took one last look at the world and went on a three week trip to Europe. It was beautiful and I became a little more in touch with my ancestral roots. It was also good testing grounds for preparing to march with heavy equipment on one's back, as I backpacked for most of the trip.

When I arrived back home I worked for a bit and then that winter it was off to basic training. During those 2 and one half years in the military I learned a lot about leadership and how to follow as well. It has prepared me mentally and physically for many trials in my life. I met many wonderful people just like in University and it helped prepare me for the next step on my life's journey.

After two years of training I finally realized that the military was not for me at least at that point in my life. Many issues were gnawing at me from back home and I could no longer focus properly to serve the way I was expected to. So I asked for a voluntary release…

Although it took 6 months, the paper work went through and I was on my way home. During this period I had time to reflect on my past and what I had done with my life. I was also being reintroduced to God, who I learned about as a child. And I could see that my life was heading down yet another path. After being released from the military I spent some time in the city I was living in at the time, looking for work, but ultimately headed back to where I was born.

The next few years were a whirlwind of events that would eventually lead me into a place I had never expected to be. I found a job in my field of work after some searching and a small spiritual break after leaving the military and finally settled in an apartment in my home town. However that did not last long and I was on my way again. Soon after being laid off, I moved back in with my mother and was working part-time in the financial industry. Little did I know my life was about to change for the better, but not before one last major detour.

I started volunteering on a farm around the same time and it was working out well, but one of the choices I made while working there landed me, eventually, behind bars. This brings us almost to the point of this study. "…all things God works for the good of those who love him…" (Romans 8:28).

The time in prison although not lengthy (6 months) compared to my entire life was significant in that I had time to reflect and reassess what direction I was travelling in. I also had time to make some concrete plans to head in the right direction, once I was released, which led to the book you are currently reading, amongst other great plans.

Although all life decisions do not always lead to an immediate "happy ever after ending", it is my hope that your decision to pick up this book is a part of yours. As I know it was a joy to write it!

Enjoy and take time to really understand your purpose here on earth.

STEP 1: Accepting God's Love

"Greater love has no one than this:
to lay down one's life for one's friends."
—JOHN 15:13

Story: Common Ground

A young man, whose life experience was going down a different road than most of his immediate family's had, had some choices to make. After years of just "getting by" in high school, he finally realized, with some help, that he needed to change his attitude and thought process if he was ever going to succeed in University.

After a year of readjusting and regaining some of the confidence of his childhood, he recognized that it was very possible to succeed and graduate where none of his family had before him.

Above all he met a friend, a teacher's aide, who would teach him things about himself and the world he never thought possible. This friend was not the same skin colour or even from the same side of the world as the student, but the bond and friendship they developed was unparalleled in this young man's life before that.

This experience goes to show you that God can work through anybody. They do not have to be the same skin colour, come from the same country or even be in the same "religion" as you are, but the bonds that are developed are very much the one's God creates between loving, caring human beings. Sometimes these bonds last a life time or only for a fleeting moment but the memories last forever.

In the epistle to the Romans it is mentioned "Indeed, when Gentiles, who do not have the law, do by nature things required by the law, they are a law for themselves, even though they do not have the law. They show that the requirements of the law are written on their hearts, their consciences also bearing witness, and their thoughts sometimes accusing them and at other times even defending them." (Romans 2:14–15)

When reading through this lesson think about the common ground one shares with other human beings from different races and religions so you can start building friendships on that truth.

Lesson: Sacrifice

Golden Rule: Do unto others as you would have done unto yourself. Every major world religion has this rule in common and a God they should love.

In Christianity all of God's laws can be wrapped up in two commandments. "Love the Lord your God with all your heart and with all your soul and with all your mind… and… Love your neighbor as yourself" (Matthew 22:37–40).

Jesus goes one further during His ministry and says "…love your enemies and pray for those who persecute you, that you may be children of your Father in heaven." (Matthew 5:44, 45).

Jesus showed all of God's love to us through His ministry:

- He preached the coming kingdom of heaven (Mark 1:15, Matthew 4:17, Luke 10:9).

- He laid His life down on the cross for us as a sinless man to take all of our sins on His life (Luke 23:33, 2 Corinthians 5:21).

- God resurrected His body after three days in a tomb so that Jesus is now alive in heaven awaiting His return to earth (Matthew 17:23).

- And to all those who believe; He gave His Holy Spirit to dwell in us until He comes with all His glory (2 Timothy 1:14, Ephesians 1:13, 14).

Jesus was tempted before His ministry began (Matthew 4:1–11). He faced trials during His ministry (Luke 22:28). And He defeated the enemy through His death and resurrection. Jesus did all of this to fulfill God's plan to save us from our sins and give us the opportunity to have the gift of eternal life in His kingdom (John 3:16).

NOTES

_____

_____

_____

_____

Discussion: Knowledge

"Where there is love there is life"
—MAHATMA GHANDI

Christ laid his life down for us in order to stand for the truth! When reading and answering questions to this step's discussion, focus on the simple things Christ did for us.

Discussion Questions

1. How do you relate your personal belief system with other religions, people and belief systems?

_____

_____

_____

_____

_____

2. Do you look for common ground with yourself and others or do you separate yourself from others based on differences?

_____

_____

_____

_____

_____

3. How can a person reconcile ones' belief system with other religions, people and belief systems? List some ideas.

_____

_____

_____

_____

_____

4. How do you relate your faith journey with respect to the roots of Christianity? That is, the people (Jesus, Paul, Peter, etc.) previously of the Jewish faith whom it was founded by. Read John 4:22 and Romans 3:1, 2 for some insight.

_____

_____

_____

_____

_____

5. Pick out at least one place in the Bible (New Testament) that suggests Jesus was a practicing Jew.

_____

_____

_____

_____

_____

STEP 2: What Should We Do?

"Yet to all who did receive him, to those who believed in his name, he gave the right to become children of God."

—JOHN 1:12

Story: Decisions

A young man who had just finished University joined the military. He had always admired leadership in his country and wanted to do his part to serve the country that had protected his right to freedom since he was a young child.

Little did he know that God had a different plan. He joined, but a couple of years in he saw that, although the forces were a great career path and a wonderful life experience, it was not for him.

After six months of mulling over options with military career staff, he finally decided to leave. Hoping and trusting in the Lord to lead him for the remainder of his life.

At times in life you are left with choices. They are not always easy, but they have to be made. If God is speaking to you, even using these pages, you probably have choices to make. Take time and "mull" over the decision(s) that might have to be made. As the Bible says, "…hasty feet miss the way." (Proverbs 19:2).

Take time, read through this lesson and ask God what He has in store for you. Make clear the decisions that appear before you!

Lesson: Acceptance

Accept God into your life. No person can make you do this; it has to be a personal decision. Accept that you are a sinner and that you do not have control over your own life (Matthew 19:17).

There are two forces at work in this world, good and evil and every day we make our choice as to which side we are going to be on, the good or the bad (Matthew 7:15–20).

If it were up to God, He would have us choose His way every day, but because He loves us so much He gave us the option to choose; His way or the way of the world (John 1:13).

Unfortunately, left to our own decisions we often choose the wrong way which separates us from Him (Mark 7:20–23). However, God never wants us to take that path (Deuteronomy 20:19).

Thank God, He knew that left to our own devices we would turn from Him. That is why He sent His only Son down to earth to be the atonement for our sins. Now all we have to do is accept Him into our life (John 10:7–17).

Praise God that Jesus, His Son, died for our sins and was raised back up to heaven, having defeated Satan and his multitudes. Do you realize this? If so you have an option. You can continue your life as you are or you can accept the blood of Jesus in your life to wash away your sins. Turn to God in earnest prayer asking Him for forgiveness, through Christ, for everything you have ever done against Him. This is called repentance (Matthew 3:2).

God is more than ready to accept your prayers for forgiveness. Jesus spoke of the lost sheep that ran away from the flock. The shepherd left the ninety-nine to save the one who was lost. This is how He feels about us (Luke 15:4–7).

NOTES

_____

_____

_____

_____

_____

_____

_____

_____

_____

_____

_____

_____

_____

Discussion: Planning

"The destiny of man is not measured by material computation, when great forces are on the move in the world, we learn we are spirits, not animals."
—Sir Winston Churchill

Soldiers of our nations are expected to make the ultimate sacrifice for their country and fellow man when asked to. Never are they asked to blindly lose their lives. They are part of a calculated and accurately made "bigger plan". When reading and answering questions to this step's discussion keep in mind what purpose God has for you in His "bigger plan".

Discussion Questions

1. What choices do you have to make in your life currently? List them out and make clear the options you could take for each of them.

_____

_____

_____

_____

_____

2. If it came down to it would you be ready to make the ultimate sacrifice for your beliefs? Why or why not?

_____

_____

_____

_____

_____

3. What changes could you make in your daily routine that would have a positive impact on you and the world around you?

_____

_____

_____

_____

_____

4. What choices have you made in the past that have changed your life, positive or negative? List them out.

_____

_____

_____

_____

_____

5. If negative, what can you do to use those negative choices and turn them into positives for yourself and others who can learn from them?

_____

_____

_____

_____

_____

STEP 3: The Right Path

*"Enter through the narrow gate. For wide is the gate and broad is
the road that leads to destruction, and many enter through it."*
—MATTHEW 7:13

Story: Revelation

A young man who had recently learned about Jesus and the
knowledge of a life after earth was stuck at a cross roads in life;
he could continue down the path to destruction or try this "new
idea" called following Jesus.

Little did he know that he still had a few hard lessons to
learn before he would completely submit his will to God. After
attending some churches and embracing his new found faith he
was sent away from fellowship. Disillusioned and upset he stopped
praying and reading the Bible and hoped that God alone would
lead him in the correct direction.

The result was a mound of debt and then jail, both of which
he had never considered, never mind experienced before in his life.

Even with these unexpected hardships he decided to "pull
up his socks" and take responsibility as he always had. He chose
to pick up the Bible and start reading again. This decision would
change the rest of his life and for the better!

Occasionally in life we hit road blocks, especially as new believers. But we must ask ourselves, "Why is this all happening?" instead of playing the blame game. Keeping a daily routine of right decisions is important and this is the beginning of the right path.

While reading through this lesson, consider the revelation that is taking place and how this fits in with your plans for the future?

Lesson: Plans

What is the right path you might ask? It is a personal and loving relationship with God, through His only begotten Son, Jesus Christ (Matthew 11:28–30). At first this path may not seem easy, as it is a "narrow gate", but those who choose to "enter through" are destined for blessings and love in this life and much more in the life to come (Luke 12:37).

The right path is no longer your path. It is the path chosen by God for you. You must choose to die to your old self, your old ways, and your old habits. By doing this you are cleansed and set apart to develop new ways and new habits (2 Corinthians 5:14–17, James 1:21). This new life of yours must be directed by God, through your prayers and praise, reading God's Word and fellowshipping with other believers (Ephesians 4:21–24, Acts 6:4).

We need to pray and give praise to God in order to keep in contact with Him and show Him our gratitude for all He has done for us (Luke 19:37, 38). You might say what has He done for me, lately? Just look around and see, the trees, the birds, shelter, family and friends, food, all created by the hands of God. Right communication with others is the key to growth on earth, why should it be any different with God? He wants to hear our prayers so that He can help us with our problems, to leave more time for us to enjoy Him and His creation. Praise God! If you ask how do we pray? Jesus says how to in Matthew 6:5–15. God says He even intercedes with groaning when we are unable to talk and knows what we need before we ask for it (Romans 8:26, Matthew 6:8). What a great God! Most importantly we need to give our complete will to God and ask that *His will be done in our lives.* As a new creation in Christ we no longer live for ourselves, but for Him (Matthew 6:10).

Now that we have an understanding of how to speak to God, how will we know what His answers are? The best way is to read His Word. Start by asking God about something you have on your mind and then simply open up the Bible to look for an answer. The great thing about God and His Holy Spirit is that He will lead you to the information you need to read. He will speak to you right from the book. This of course takes faith and you have to believe that the Bible is the inspired Word of God and not just written by some men over the last 4,000 years or so (2 Timothy 3:16). However, once you do, you will find a great comfort in knowing that He is and always will be with you (Romans 5:5).

Understanding and reading on your own is a great start, but the only way to fully appreciate and feel the joy, peace and happiness of God is to visit and fellowship with other believers who share your passion and love for our Almighty Creator. As the old saying goes, "Iron sharpens iron" (Proverbs 27:17). In order to find a place that is right for you it may take a while. There are many different ways of worshipping our God. No one is better than the other; however, one may better fit your character and up bringing than another. But never lose sight of the main reason of fellowship and that is to come together and worship our God in unity (1 Corinthians 1:9). Take your time and visit various churches, make sure that they preach salvation in Jesus Christ (2 Timothy 2:10). And lastly, ask God to help find the right one for you!

NOTES

_____

_____

_____

_____

_____

_____

_____

_____

_____

_____

_____

_____

_____

_____

_____

Discussion: Change

"We have learned to turn out lots of goods and services, but we haven't learned as well how to have everybody share in the bounty. The obligation of a society as prosperous as ours is to figure out how nobody gets left to far behind."
—WARREN BUFFET

Business men require a plan in order to succeed at what they want to do. They could be selling any old widget, but if Business Man A is selling the same widget as Business Man B, and Business Man B has a well thought out plan, he is more likely to succeed. When reading and answering questions to this step's discussion make sure that the plans you are developing for your future in Christ are well thought out and led by Him alone!

Discussion Questions

1. No matter what you choose to do in life, whether it is plans to become a billionaire or plans to change the way you live your day to day life, it takes hard work, determination and perseverance. What are a couple of choices you can make or change in your daily routine to start down or better follow the right path?

_____

_____

_____

_____

_____

2. "Right communication" is the key to growth here on earth and above. What types of changes can you make in your communication with others and God in order to "prosper" on your trip down the right path?

_____

_____

_____

_____

_____

3. Giving praise to God is the same as saying thank you! Before moving on with your plans in your new life, write a list of things you have to be thankful for past, present and then into the future!

_____

_____

_____

_____

_____

STEP 4: Restoring Relationships

*"…turn the hearts of the parents to their children
and the disobedient to the wisdom of the righteous—
to make ready a people prepared for the Lord."*
—LUKE 1:17

Story: Forgiveness

A boy who had lived his life like most of the other boys in his neighbourhood decided that he wanted to do more with what he had. He had big dreams and they continued to grow larger as he did.

However one day as a young man he realized that there had to be more to life than striving for earthly gain.

He decided to go back to the church of his boyhood and start searching for answers. This decision was the beginning of the dream he was looking for.

Along with the joy of finding likeminded caring people, he also realized he had made many mistakes as a young child and adult that he needed forgiveness for.

This was the start of his path to restoring relationships with the people in his life and God.

Your story might be similar to this one. Take time to read

this chapter and figure out what might be holding you back from accomplishing the dream God has for you!

Lesson: Coming home

Just like restoring our relationship with our Father in heaven, it is important that we take a long look at our past relationships with family, friends, co-workers, coaches, pastors, partners, teachers and the list will go on. How are our relationships or how were they? Do they need some repair? Do some emotional ties need to be let go or angry words need to be forgiven? Not only has Jesus become our advocate to reconnect with our Father in heaven, He has also done the same to restore our relationships on earth with others we may have hurt or others who may have hurt us in the past (2 Corinthians 5:18, 19).

A perfect example is the parable of the prodigal son. Jesus talks of a young man who wants to have his portion of the inheritance while his father is still alive. He is given his share and spends it recklessly in a faraway country on women and partying. He ends up working on a farm for next to no money and comes to the realization that he is being treated no better than the pigs, where he could be back on his dad's farm working for at least a fair wage. He decides to go home and reconcile with his father, who receives him with open arms and a feast. His brother, who stayed home, is jealous at first, but never the less the family is together again (Luke 15:11–32). The point of this story is to let us know that we have all made mistakes and have caused broken relationships, but no matter what, there is always an opportunity to change and make good what was once wrong.

How do we restore those relationships? First, a broken relationship from our past may have taken years or our whole lives to develop. Come to realize it will not take over night to feel like you once did and the relationship may never be the way it once was. The most important thing is that we become clear minded, forgiving and except forgiveness for whatever has happened in the past to us and the other(s) involved (Mark 11:25).

Most broken relationships are a result of a break in *trust* of the other person(s) involved. This could be due to any number of reasons, which are, cheating, abuse, jealousy, lying, hatred and the list goes on. If the other person(s) involved does not have the tools to forgive, you must know that what is most important is that God has forgiven you already. That is the perfect sacrifice Jesus Christ made for us (Romans 5:8). Understand that you will never find the soul fulfilling love from any individual here on earth, like the love from our Father in heaven (Psalm 18:30).

How many times should we forgive? We might say, but this person hurt me so many times, how could I ever forgive them? Jesus says to forgive not seven times, but seventy times seven (Matthew 18:21–35). Or they did a horrible thing that could never be forgiven. Believe it! Jesus Christ died for those sins too! Anything against God is sin no matter how big or small it is to our eyes and mind or society as a whole. God does not treat one person any greater than another (Romans 2:11).

NOTES

_____

_____

_____

_____

_____

_____

_____

_____

_____

_____

_____

_____

_____

_____

_____

_____

_____

_____

_____

Discussion: Mending

*"I learned that courage was not the absence of fear, but
the triumph over it. The brave man is not he who does
not feel afraid, but he who conquers that fear."*
—NELSON MANDELA

Politicians are required to do many jobs. They must be business
minded, family oriented, diplomatic and self-sacrificing in time
and efforts for "the greater good". When reading and answering
questions to this step's discussion keep in mind the type of person
you want to become and how this affects your relationships with
others.

Discussion Questions

1. Nelson Mandela went through many trials in his life,
    including 27 years in jail, but he persevered to help create
    independence for his people. Your life's trials may not be
    as extreme as Mr. Mandela's but never the less you have
    likely gone through rough times. What is holding you
    back from taking your next step in life's journey? Write
    a list of people you need to forgive and write down any
    words of concern or issues that need to be discussed in
    each circumstance in order to restore that relationship and
    move on in your new life.

---

2. What other steps can you take to mend the relationships and move on in your new life with God and others?

_____

_____

_____

_____

_____

3. What steps can you take to mend your relationship with God if you have been far from him in the past?

_____

_____

_____

_____

_____

STEP 5: Staying On the Path

*"Whoever wants to be my disciple must deny themselves
and take up their cross daily and follow me."*
—LUKE 9:23

Story: Faith

A woman who was raised during a time of world turmoil and trouble learned to live modestly during times of plenty.

She lived in less than ideal housing conditions as a child and learned to make do with what she had.

As this woman grew older she survived through many other trials with family and friends, but she always stayed on the path God had set for her.

Sometimes staying on the path can be challenging, especially when we have to forgive people from our past and trust that God has full control over the situation, past, present, and future. But once we have submitted ourselves to God's plan it makes helping carry it out much easier. As the Bible says, "take up" your "cross daily" (Luke 9:23).

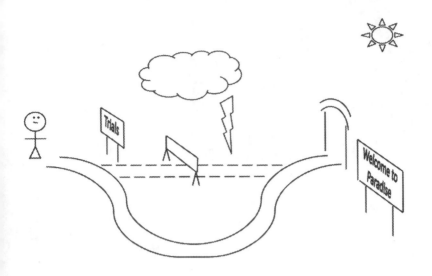

Lesson: Staying True

If you have made it this far, congratulations! Although the subject in this chapter is simple to understand it is crucial in our ability to maintain our new life. We had discussed in Lesson 3 what the right path is, now we will discuss how to stay on it (2 Corinthians 11:3). Most importantly we must fall asleep at night and wake up every day with God on our minds. We must ask ourselves in the morning, what will God have me do today? And pray about it (Jeremiah 10:23). Before we go to bed we must ask God to bring us to rest, ask for forgiveness for whatever we might have done wrong today and thank Him for everything He has given us (Ephesians 4:26).

Remember, whatever happened in our past has been forgiven and it is now time to move on in our new life with Jesus Christ and God the Father. We must put away our old selves and start developing new characteristics, God's characteristics, new habits, new friends and new places of work and commune (Ephesians 4:22). The only way to live this new life is to turn from the old one!

Spending time with God daily is important, not only in prayer, but also in His Word. Pick up the Bible in the morning before you start your day and spend a few minutes grounding yourself in His Word. Do the same thing at night. You will be amazed at how much change comes and how quickly when you are obeying God (Colossians 3:16).

Seek out people who are like minded, who have a thirst and hunger for God like you do. You do not have to spend every day with them, but keep them in your prayers and on your heart (2 Corinthians 6:14).

Lastly, as a new believer, we may start developing idea's that are not biblically sound and take scripture too literal when we study His Word alone. Although every piece of scripture has its purpose we must remember through prayer and speaking with others about God, we will learn much more for ourselves (Proverbs 3:7). And, we must ask questions and prove what is the Truth for ourselves (1 Thessalonians 5:21).

NOTES

_____

_____

_____

_____

_____

_____

_____

_____

_____

Discussion: Strength

"A clear and innocent conscience fears nothing"
—Queen Elizabeth I

Royalty must be an example for the people they reign over. The nation they represent requires of them to be soldier like, business minded, politically involved, but above all they usually have a certain amount of devout faith to their countries common spiritual beliefs. When reading and answering questions to this step's discussion keep in mind the type of relationship you would like to maintain with God in the long term situation here on earth and ever after.

Discussion Questions

1. Queen Elizabeth I was required to be an example for a nation. She may not have been perfect, but she persevered through some of the toughest times of the 20th century. What are some of the right habits we can do on a daily basis to stay on the right path? Write them down.

_____

_____

_____

_____

_____

2. The Bible suggests that a person should pray without ceasing (1 Thessalonians 5:17). What does this mean for you? And develop a list of people, situations and life events you can pray for throughout the day.

_____

_____

_____

_____

_____

3. How can you pray throughout the day without others openly knowing about it?

_____

_____

_____

_____

_____

STEP 6: Helping Others to See

"The Spirit of the Lord is on me, because he has anointed me to proclaim good news …"
—LUKE 4:18

Story: Act it out

A husband and wife recently moved to a new neighbourhood with their children and decided to do what they thought was their Chrisitian duty by giving some neighbourly advice to the wayward neighbours. Not realizing it at the time this advice was not taken to kindly and it ended up reflecting back on the couple. After some discussion it was decided that they would act out the Christian life style rather than suggest it to others.

Some times in life it is better just to mind your own business rather than stick your nose in other peoples. The Bible mentions in 1 Thessalonians 4:11, "to lead a quiet life: You should mind your own business and work with your hands..." This would have been grand advice for this couple had they been completely submissive to God and obeying His word. However sometimes in life it is better to go through a trial and learn from it, rather than read about someone else's mistake and learn, as real life experience always stick with a person longer and deeper than fantasy...

Lesson: Giving

At first, the path we have chosen may not seem easy. Deciding to follow Christ takes dedication day after day. Sometimes we slip up, but in the end He is always there for us (2 Corinthians 12:9). We are asked to become images of Christ as we were created physical images from the beginning (Genesis 1:26). But now we must look at our inward man and clean it out, so that we can show others through our change in character who Christ really is (Romans 7:22).

Now more than ever it is important to show Christ's character in us, because a world gone seemingly awry is on a downward spiral to destruction if something does not change and soon (Hebrews 10:25). As men and women of God we must be set apart from the world, there must be a difference in us noticeable enough for someone to ask. What is the hope that is in you (1 Peter 3:15)? And our answer must be Jesus Christ.

God loves a cheerful giver and there are many ways to reach out to others that are in need (2 Corinthians 9:7). We can donate food to the poor, pray for healing of the sick, become friends with someone we may never have cared for in the past, share our testimony and at any time pray for others who are in need (Ephesians 4:28). This is God's way and it is now our way. We have a giving God, look around at everything He has provided for us and know that we must reflect that giving nature in us (Matthew 6:26). Praise the Lord!

A very important area of life where we can show others the Way is our family. Although some of our family members may not be believers, we must still love them just the same (Luke 6:27, 28). We must now become the responsible ones in showing others how to live a just life (Luke 12:48). We must walk the talk (1 Thessalonians 4:11, 12). Even Jesus was responsible for His mother until His death and then entrusted her life over to one of His followers, John (John 19:26, 27).

Most importantly, we must; lead by example, love God, worship Him, and give Him the glory in our lives (Revelation 19:1). And love our neighbours as ourselves (Galatians 5:14).

NOTES

_____

_____

_____

_____

_____

_____

_____

_____

_____

_____

_____

Discussion: Ideas

*"Peace cannot be kept by force. It can only
be achieved by understanding."*
—ALBERT EINSTEIN

Intellectually gifted people are in a league of their own. Sometimes their ideas are so forward thinking that very few others believe what these individuals are suggesting could come true. These intellects are required to believe in the unseen, much like Christians are to hope in the unseen. When reading and answering the questions to this step's discussions take time to close your eyes and envision plans God may have for you in the future.

Discussion Questions

1. Albert Einstein lived a life of servitude. He dedicated his life to the sciences and helped save the Allied countries from much unnecessary destruction during WWII. How can you walk your Christian walk by doing rather than speaking what you believe is a proper religious perspective? Develop a list of ideas.

_____

_____

_____

_____

_____

2. As Einstein said, understanding is the key to peace. To go further than that read Ecclesiastes 12:12, 13 and reflect on what can be done to help others to see.

_____

_____

_____

_____

_____

3. List some ideas of what you think God is putting on your heart to do in this new life with Christ. Remember no idea too big or too small is unimportant (Zechariah 4:10).

_____

_____

_____

_____

_____

STEP 7: Finishing the Race

"Therefore, since we are surrounded by such a great cloud of witnesses, let us throw off everything that hinders and the sin that so easily entangles. And let us run with perseverance the race marked out for us,"
—HEBREWS 12:1

Story: Endurance

A boy who was raised on a farm did not always have an easy life growing up, as he and his family went through difficult times during his childhood. As he was becoming of age the war effort was starting up. He decided he was going to do his part for his country. He left a boy but came back a man.

Upon coming back he settled in his home town and married his high school sweetheart. The two went on to have many beautiful children and grandchildren. He worked for a local car manufacturing company most of his life and did what he could for his community. Yes this man's life was not always easy.

As this man grew older he moved slower, but his wife and children, especially his wife, were always with him. This man did not spend every Sunday at church or preach out loud to his children, wife, or neighbours, but he led the Christian life the best he knew how, with a quiet confidence until the day he died.

As a Christian it is our duty to walk our own Christian walk similar to what this man did. Remember, it is not the material things on earth we can take with us, but the eternal things; love, kindness, peace, joy, goodness, and patience that God cares about (Galatians 5:22).

Lesson: Patience

My friends, this is just the beginning of a glorious and joyful life in Christ Jesus, our Lord and Saviour. Who was, is, and is yet to come (Revelation 1:8). He will never let you down. He will always be there for you when it seems no one else is (Psalm 27:1). You may go through trials and tribulations, however remember that our reward is not here on earth, but up in heaven with God (Matthew 5:12).

In order to run the race we must pace ourselves, patience is the key to our success in Christ Jesus. We did not come to this point in our lives overnight and it will take our whole lives to complete the work God is doing in us (James 1:4). And God only knows what more He will have prepared for us to do in heaven (1 Corinthians 2:9).

In order for Him to reveal more knowledge to us of His plan we must become obedient to Him in all areas of our lives, no matter how difficult it may be to let go of our past. The way to God's heart is by listening to Him (Romans 6:16). He is that still small voice among a world of confusion (1 Kings 19:12).

Finally, our life and liberty are in Jesus Christ. He has set us free from the bondage of our former life (Galatians 5:1). So let us set aside all burdens and sin and run with endurance the race that is set before us, so that on our final day we can say "I have fought the good fight, I have finished the race, I have kept the faith." (2 Timothy 4:7). To God be the Glory!

NOTES

_____

_____

_____

_____

_____

_____

_____

_____

_____

_____

_____

_____

_____

_____

_____

Discussion: Life

> *"In the end, it's not the years in your life that count. It's the life in your years."*
> —Abraham Lincoln

Visionaries, although they may have accomplished some great feat or led society in some great movement are essentially the same as the practical man next door, who plants his garden in the spring, cultivates it throughout the summer and harvests in the fall. They plant seeds, cultivate them and then watch them grow until harvest time. When reading and answering the questions to this step's discussion take time to meditate on and begin nurturing the seeds that have been planted on your heart, so that during harvest time your crop will be plenty!

Discussion Questions

1. Overall each of the leaders mentioned throughout the discussion sections have had some characteristics in common. Perseverance, courage, and a common concern for others. Another major trait that leaders require is vision. Many visions are mentioned throughout the Bible and every leader of this world requires a vision of some sort to lead a group of people to a goal. Take some time and ask God what your vision might be. Draw it out and start writing ideas down on how you may accomplish this vision.

_____

_____

_____

_____

_____

2. In continuing your journey in life and forming your relationships with others and God, what qualities or characteristics would you like to strengthen or remove from your own life in order to develop a better self? List them out and pray about how to develop those qualities you want and get rid of the ones you do not want.

_____

_____

_____

_____

_____

Reader's Guide:
How to use this book

This book was created as a compilation of steps with a short story, Bible study lesson, and discussion questions included in each step in order to provoke thought and opportunity for personal growth in Christ and in a group environment. It is meant for readers of various levels of education so that anyone can have the opportunity to better themselves.

The short stories are used to connect the reader to real life situations of trials and triumphs that take place in our daily lives.

The lesson sections are used to ground the reader in the written word of God in order to lead the reader's daily life with suggestions on how to start or restart one's daily relationships with God and others.

The discussion question sections are used to spark spiritual character development in individual readers and with others in order to help bring the stories and lessons of the Bible to the realities of daily life here on earth. The discussion answers added to some of the questions following are not exhaustive. They are meant for groups and individuals to meditate on and use as they see fit to initiate and develop self-reflection and discussion. The prayer topics are there to help start self-reflection and group prayer as seen fit by those using it.

The main focus of this book is restoring relationships, both with God and others. To this end it is my hope that anyone who takes on a leadership role in sharing the teachings in this book focuses heavily on the magnificent restoring powers of God!

STEP 1: Accepting God's Love— Reader's Guide

Discussion: Knowledge

> *"Where there is love there is life"*
> —MAHATMA GHANDI

Christ laid his life down for us in order to stand for the truth! When reading and answering questions to this step's discussion, focus on the simple things Christ did for us. The discussion answers added to some of the questions below are not exhaustive. They are meant for groups and individuals to meditate on and use as they see fit to initiate and develop self-reflection and discussion.

Discussion Questions

1. *How do you relate your personal belief system with other religions, people and belief systems?*

Encourage self-reflection and group discussion.

2. *Do you look for common ground with yourself and others or do you separate yourself from others based on differences?*

Encourage self-reflection and group discussion. Read Exodus 22:21, Ephesians 6:5 – 9

Alienation can take place very easily in this world. We are told numerous times in the Bible to take care of our slaves, and those foreigners who live in our country. As a society we must look past colour and culture and take a look at the deep rooted commonalities we all have; hunger and thirst, a desire for knowledge and better quality of life, care and concern for elders and children, etc.

These common needs and desires should bring people of different cultures and skin colour together under any nation's flag!

3. *How can a person reconcile ones' belief system with other religions, people and belief systems? List some ideas.*

Encourage self-reflection and group discussion. Readers can look to the Golden Rule for a start.

4. *How do you relate your faith journey with respect to the roots of Christianity? That is, the people (Jesus, Paul, Peter, etc.) previously of the Jewish faith whom it was founded by.*

Encourage self-reflection and group discussion. Read John 4:22 and Romans 3:1, 2 "Salvation is from the Jews".

Mainstream Christianity celebrates the Sabbath on Sunday. However some Christian groups and Judaism celebrate the Sabbath on Saturday. The military has a saying "a C is a P and the weekends are free", meaning in training a "C" grade is a pass and you have the weekends off! Western governments have a similar philosophy with closing up offices during the weekend.

The Christian realm might do well to integrate these government philosophies so as to not step on each other's toes when it comes to arguing about specific doctrines. Above putting a certain day aside for rest, let us "rejoice in the Lord always" (Philippians 4:4)!

5. *Pick out at least one place in the New Testament that suggests Jesus was a practicing Jew.*

Encourage self-reflection and group discussion. Read John 7 to start.

Prayer: Topic Suggestions

- Love
- Sacrifice
- Forgiveness
- Elderly, fatherless, widows and poor
- Unity in diversity

STEP 2: What Should We Do?— Reader's Guide

Discussion: Planning

> *"The destiny of man is not measured by material computation, when great forces are on the move in the world, we learn we are spirits, not animals."*
> —SIR WINSTON CHURCHILL

Soldiers of our nations are expected to make the ultimate sacrifice for their country and fellow man when asked to. Never are they asked to blindly lose their lives. They are part of a calculated and accurately made "bigger plan". When reading and answering questions to this step's discussion keep in mind what purpose God has for you in His "bigger plan". The discussion answers added to some of the questions below are not exhaustive. They are meant for groups and individuals to meditate on and use as they see fit to initiate and develop self-reflection and discussion.

Discussion Questions

1. *What choices do you have to make in your life currently? List them out and make clear the options you can take for each of them.*

Encourage self-reflection and group discussion. Examples may include, looking for a new job, buying a new home, buying a new car, changing various personal relationship situations, accepting Christ as ruler of our life, etc.

2. *If it came down to it would you be ready to make the ultimate sacrifice for your beliefs? Why or why not?*

Encourage self-reflection and group discussion.

3. *What changes can you make in your daily routine that will have a positive impact on you and the world around you?*

Encourage self-reflection and group discussion. Examples may include, reading the Bible or praying more often, etc.

4. *What choices have you made in the past that have changed your life, positive or negative? List them out.*

Encourage self-reflection and group discussion.

5. *If negative, what can you do to use those negative choices and turn them into positives for yourself and others who can learn from them?*

Encourage self-reflection and group discussion. An example would be over drinking often, which negatively affects performance levels in completing daily tasks. The positive would be stopping the negative habit and talking to others who have the same problem, encouraging them that they too can free themselves of the overindulging habit.

Prayer: Topic Suggestions

- Acceptance
- Government/Authority
- Military Service Members
- Discernment
- Decisions

STEP 3: The Right Path— Reader's Guide

Discussion: Change

> *"We have learned to turn out lots of goods and services, but we haven't learned as well how to have everybody share in the bounty. The obligation of a society as prosperous as ours is to figure out how nobody gets left to far behind."*
> —WARREN BUFFET

Business men require a plan in order to succeed at what they want to do. They could be selling any old widget, but if Business Man A is selling the same widget as Business Man B, and Business Man B has a well thought out plan, he is more likely to succeed. When reading and answering questions to this step's discussion make sure that the plans you are developing for your future in Christ are well thought out and led by Him alone! The discussion answers added to some of the questions below are not exhaustive. They are meant for groups and individuals to meditate on and use as they see fit to initiate and develop self-reflection and discussion.

Discussion Questions

1. *No matter what you choose to do in life, whether it is plans to become a billionaire or plans to change the way you live your day to day life, it takes hard work, determination and perseverance. What are a couple of choices you can make or change in your daily routine to start down or better follow the right path?*

Encourage self-reflection and group discussion. In regards to the Bible study lesson you should, Pray, Read the Bible, Fellowship and Worship God. However this is not an exhaustive list of changes especially for anyone who has developed "bad habits" throughout life. Other changes may include, drinking less alcohol, acting more mercifully, spending more time with loved ones, etc.

2. *"Right communication" is the key to growth here on earth and above. What types of changes can you make in your communication with others and God in order to "prosper" on your trip down the right path?*

Encourage self-reflection and group discussion.

3. *Giving praise to God is the same as saying thank you! Before moving on with your plans in your new life, write a list of things you have to be thankful for past, present and then into the future!*

Encourage self-reflection and group discussion. And don't just be thankful for the good things. Read 1 Thessalonians 5:18 and Philippians 4 for more insight.

Prayer: Topic Suggestions

- Community Prosperity
- Direction
- Thankfulness
- Wisdom
- Patience

STEP 4: Restoring Relationships— Reader's Guide

Discussion: Mending

> *"I learned that courage was not the absence of fear, but the triumph over it. The brave man is not he who does not feel afraid, but he who conquers that fear."*
> —NELSON MANDELA

Politicians are required to do many jobs. They must be business minded, family oriented, diplomatic and self-sacrificing in time and efforts for "the greater good". When reading and answering questions to this step's discussion keep in mind the type of person you want to become and how this affects your relationships with others. The discussion answers added to some of the questions below are not exhaustive. They are meant for groups and individuals to meditate on and use as they see fit to initiate and develop self-reflection and discussion.

Discussion Questions

1. *Nelson Mandela went through many trials in his life, including 27 years in jail, but he persevered to help create independence for his people. Your life's trials may not be as extreme as Mr. Mandela's but never the less you have likely gone through rough times. What is holding you back from taking your next step in life's journey? Write a list of people you need to forgive and write down any words of concern or issues that need to be discussed in each circumstance in order to restore that relationship and move on in your new life.*

Encourage self-reflection and group discussion. As in the study the list may include, teachers, co-workers, friends, family, partners, etc. Exhaust the list in order to bring to light the people and issues involved.

Remember these issues did not crop up overnight. Take time to confront each concern and person.

You may find in some circumstances the other party involved never thought about the issue. However what is most important is that YOU are moving on in your new life with Christ.

2. *What other steps can you take to mend the relationships and move on in your new life with God and others?*

Encourage self-reflection and group discussion. Read Matthew 18

3. *What steps can you take to mend your relationship with God if you have been far from him in the past?*

Encourage self-reflection and group discussion. Pray, Read God's Word, Praise God and Fellowship. Review Step 3 Lesson for more. And remember that each person is at a different stage in their journey with God, so be patient.

Prayer: Topic Suggestions

- Family
- Friends
- Coworkers
- Reconciliation
- Patience

STEP 5: Staying On the Path—Reader's Guide

Discussion: Strength

"A clear and innocent conscience fears nothing"
—QUEEN ELIZABETH I

Royalty must be an example for the people they reign over. The nation they represent requires of them to be soldier like, business minded, politically involved, but above all they usually have a certain amount of devout faith to their countries common spiritual beliefs. When reading and answering questions to this step's discussion keep in mind the type of relationship you would like to maintain with God in the long term situation here on earth and ever after. The discussion answers added to some of the questions below are not exhaustive. They are meant for groups and individuals to meditate on and use as they see fit to initiate and develop self-reflection and discussion.

Discussion Questions

1.   *Queen Elizabeth I was required to be an example for a nation. She may not have been perfect, but she persevered through some of the toughest times of the 20th century. What are some of the right habits we can do on a daily basis to stay on the right path? Write them down.*

Encourage self-reflection and group discussion. Review Step 3: Question 1, and revamp your answers as needed, for a renewed look at how you would like to spend your daily life here on earth with others and in a continually strengthened relationship with God. Again, every life in a relationship with God should be grounded in His Word, prayer, fellowship and worship daily.

2.   *The Bible suggests that a person should pray without ceasing (1 Thessalonians 5:17). What does this mean for you? Develop a list of people, situations and life events you can pray for throughout your day.*

Encourage self-reflection and group discussion. Ceasing means "to stop", so without ceasing means without stopping. We are encouraged by the words of the Bible to never stop praying, morning, afternoon and night, in shopping lines, out for dinner at a restaurant, and at work. We should be continually praying for the people around us, life events and for the situations we walk into, etc.

Also keep in mind that praying is like having a conversation with another person. God does not need you to be detailed and "wordy". All he wants to hear is what is on your mind, because he already knows (Matthew 9:4). The simplest prayer to do is "Your will be done God". Sometimes we have other types of conversations with God that are more heartfelt and involve tears, but that is where the closet comes in to play (Matthew 6:6). Remember, prayer is like talking with other humans, often it is very gentle and simple requests, but there are times of frustration, disappointment, defeat and severe repentance that is required.

3. *How can you pray throughout the day without others openly knowing about it?*

Encourage self-reflection and group discussion. Keep in mind, it's possible to pray with your eyes open and mouth closed, but it takes some practice.

Prayer: Topic Suggestions

- Mercy
- Respect
- Loyalty
- Courage
- Endurance

STEP 6: Helping Others to See—Reader's Guide

Discussion: Ideas

> *"Peace cannot be kept by force. It can only be achieved by understanding."*
> —ALBERT EINSTEIN

Intellectually gifted people are in a league of their own. Sometimes their ideas are so forward thinking that very few others believe what these individuals are suggesting could come true. These intellects are required to believe in the unseen, much like Christians are to hope in the unseen. When reading and answering the questions to this step's discussions take time to close your eyes and envision plans God may have for you in the future. The discussion answers added to some of the questions below are not exhaustive. They are meant for groups and individuals to meditate on and use as they see fit to initiate and develop self-reflection and discussion.

Discussion Questions

1. *Albert Einstein lived a life of servitude. He dedicated his life to the sciences and helped save the Allied countries from much unnecessary destruction during WWII. How can you walk your Christian walk by doing rather than speaking what you believe is a proper religious perspective? Develop a list of ideas you believe God is putting on your heart to do in order to show others who Christ is.*

Encourage self-reflection and group discussion. To get started suggestions made in the Bible study are: pray for others, feed the poor, talk to others you may never have before. Remember, leading by example is the best way to show others who Christ really is. As the Bible says, "work out your salvation with fear and trembling" (Philippians 2:12).

2. *As Einstein said, understanding is the key to peace. To go further than that read Ecclesiastes 12:12, 13 and reflect on what can be done to help others to see.*

Encourage self-reflection and group discussion. As Ecclesiastes 12:12, 13 suggests fear God and listen to Him.

3. *List some ideas of what you think God is putting on your heart to do in this new life with Christ. Remember no idea too big or too small is unimportant (Zechariah 4:10).*

Encourage self-reflection and group discussion. Some ideas are finding a new job, picking up an old hobby, sharing more time with family, etc.

Prayer: Topic Suggestions

- Understanding
- Acceptance
- Patience
- Perseverance
- Fellowship

STEP 7: Finishing the Race—Reader's Guide

Discussion: Life

> *"In the end, it's not the years in your life that count. It's the life in your years."*
> —ABRAHAM LINCOLN

Visionaries, although they may have accomplished some great feat or led society in some great movement are essentially the same as the practical man next door, who plants his garden in the spring, cultivates it throughout the summer and harvests in the fall. They plant seeds, cultivate them and then watch them grow until harvest time. When reading and answering the questions to this step's discussion take time to meditate on and begin nurturing the seeds that have been planted on your heart, so that during harvest time your crop will be plenty! The discussion answers added to some of the questions below are not exhaustive. They are meant for groups and individuals to meditate on and use as they see fit to initiate and develop self-reflection and discussion.

Discussion Questions

1. *Overall each of the leaders mentioned throughout the discussion sections have had some characteristics in common. Perseverance, courage, and a common concern for others. Another major trait that leaders require is vision. Many visions are mentioned throughout the Bible and every leader of this world requires a vision of some sort to lead a group of people to a goal. Take some time and ask God what your vision might be. Draw it out and start writing ideas down on how you may accomplish this vision.*

Encourage self-reflection and group discussion. The vision that is developing in your mind may be as simple as starting to learn a new language or as big as starting your own business. Nurture your vision and in time it will develop to what you want it to be. Remember every great accomplishment in this world started with an idea, a seed, a VISION! As President Lincoln said "It's the LIFE in your years" that are important.

2. *In continuing your journey in life and forming your relationships with others and God, what qualities or characteristics would you like to strengthen or remove from your own life in order to develop a better self? List them out and pray about how to develop those qualities you want and get rid of the ones you do not want.*

Encourage self-reflection and group discussion. The key to growth in Christ is getting rid of the old person. It is a lifelong practice and unfortunately you may maintain some of the scars from your past for your entire life. However those scars need not be burdens, but only reminders of your temporal body and what it has been through to prepare yourself for a much greater purpose for eternity! When developing your list, think seriously about the person you want to become in the long-term. Character traits such as honesty, loyalty, patience, joyfulness, courage and strength through Christ are qualities you might want to consider in your journey to your happily ever after!

Prayer: Topic Suggestions

- Endurance
- Provisions
- Opportunities
- Charity
- Servitude

NOTES

NOTES

NOTES

NOTES

THE
SINAI
EXPERIENCE

A Forty Day Devotional

ADONA THOMPSON

WESTBOW *
PRESS
A DIVISION OF THOMAS NELSON
& ZONDERVAN

Scripture taken from the New King James Version. Copyright 1979, 1980,
1982 by Thomas Nelson, inc. Used by permission. All rights reserved.

Scripture taken from the King James Version of the Bible.

Scripture quotations taken from the Holy Bible, New Living
Translation, copyright 1996, 2004. Used by permission of Tyndale
House Publishers, Inc., Wheaton, Illinois 60189. All rights reserved.

WestBow Press books may be ordered through
booksellers or by contacting:

WestBow Press
A Division of Thomas Nelson & Zondervan
1663 Liberty Drive
Bloomington, IN 47403
www.westbowpress.com
1 (866) 928-1240

Because of the dynamic nature of the Internet, any web addresses or
links contained in this book may have changed since publication and
may no longer be valid. The views expressed in this work are solely those
of the author and do not necessarily reflect the views of the publisher,
and the publisher hereby disclaims any responsibility for them.

Any people depicted in stock imagery provided by Thinkstock are
models, and such images are being used for illustrative purposes only.
Certain stock imagery © Thinkstock.

ISBN: 978-1-4908-2581-6 (sc)

Library of Congress Control Number: 2014902318

Printed in the United States of America.

WestBow Press rev. date: 03/31/2014

ACKNOWLEDGEMENTS

I give God thanks for placing in me the courage to write and for all the great people He has given to me to see His will accomplished. To my husband, I am truly grateful for your passionate support, giving me the tools to put faith in action and for loving me the way you do. To Hermion Cheddick for your selflessness and passion to see the will of God accomplish in the life of others. Thank you for being the one through whom this devotional can easily be published. To my daughter, your smiles speak volumes to me. Keep smiling. To my Pastor, Reverend Phillip Chase, your words of encouragement challenged me to be persistent in God. Thank you for your great spiritual leadership.

FOREWORD

Getting out of Egypt is one task, but getting Egypt out of you is an even greater task. Egypt usually refers to sin, bondage, and the world. It required the ultimate sacrifice of the Lamb of God to bring deliverance to all who believe on Him. After salvation, walking in the freedom that Jesus has bought through His blood can be a struggle for believers. The Sinai experience addresses the struggles that believers may have in their journey and it also seeks to reveal the character of Christ, so that in the midst of your personal Sinai Experience, you can see God for who He is.

He is the God of man, the only one we should serve. He fashioned man in His likeness and gave him the option to live in obedience to Him. The word of God has great impact on man; it is what we hear from God's word that will bring life to our faith (**Authorised King James Version Bible)**, **Romans 10:17**" but we begin by hearing, trusting and confessing. When Moses heard the voice of God at Sinai, his faith came alive. There was no doubt in his heart that it was the voice of God. The Spirit of God started to move in his life, just like He does in ours, starting a fire within, that will not consume us but will be the beginning of a relationship that will change our lives forever. The truth is not just what we hear, but it is the living reality of the true and living God. When truth has gotten a hold of our lives, we will understand the relevance of the statutes of God laid down in the Old Testament and the reality of His love. Jesus is the fulfillment of the law, the love of God expressed to mankind, the opening and closing of the letter. His death, burial and resurrection openly confirm to all who hear, that indeed, truth is come to make men free.

You, who have come out of Egypt, be assured that He who brought you out of Egypt will take you to the Promised Land. Jesus prayed, (***Authorised King James Version Bible, John 17:15&17***) "I pray not that thou shouldest take them out of the world, but that thou shouldest keep them from the evil…sanctify them through thy truth: thy word is truth". A delightful walk with God and His word is a great step into victorious Christian living, impacting the world through Him.

INTRODUCTION

Sinai is found in the wilderness of Paran and was first
mentioned in (*Authorised King James Version Bible,* Genesis
Chapter 21:21)

Hagar and her son Ishmael were sent into exile there. It
became a very prominent feature in Israel's history, because
it was there God gave to Moses the Ten Commandments.
"The Sinai Experience" focuses on the book of Exodus,
supported by other books of the **B**ible, which reveals the
power of God in delivering His people from bondage and
leading them into the Promised Land. It is a great analogy
to what happens in the lives of believers today. The Lord
Saves and delivers, but there is an ongoing war against the
kingdom of darkness. We would have victory when we
put all our confidence in God.

I was preparing a Sunday School lesson, taken from
Exodus Chapter three (3) in October 2007 when this
verse of scripture in (*Authorised King James Version Bible*
Exodus 3:12) which says "And he said, Certainly I will
be with thee; and this shall be a token unto thee, that I
have sent thee: When thou hast brought forth the people
out of Egypt, ye shall serve God upon this mountain"

leaped out at me. I pondered on this verse for a while and asked myself the question, what is God really calling His servants to do? I realized that the call to service is a call to totally depend on God; to sit, to listen, to learn, to be lead by God, so that you can effectively lead others. Moses service to God, recorded in the first five books of the Bible; Genesis (the revelation of beginnings), Exodus (separation unto God), Leviticus (Law of the priest), Numbers (the book of journeying) and Deuteronomy (The book of remembrances), became an eternal blessing to Israel, and the world. I hope that as you take time to spend with God you will find a place of rest in Him.

CONTENTS

HE IS THE SOURCE OF LIVING WATERS

Genesis 21:15-21. *(New King James Version (NKJV). "Then God opened her eyes and she saw a well of water, and she filled the skin with water, and gave the lad a drink".*

God is filled with compassion. In the Book of Genesis 21:15-21,NKJV He heard the cry of a rejected woman and her son. Sometimes, the pain of rejection can be severe because it is a yearning to be loved, to know that someone cares. There is one who feels our deepest pain and understands the cry of every human heart. So, God revealed himself to Hagar and showed her that she can depend on him. Jesus said to the Samaritan woman at the well, "Give me a drink". She later discovered that He who was speaking to her, was the source of living waters (John 4:14, NKJV). There may be dry, deserted, areas in our lives: areas of heart break, condemnation, bitterness and unhappiness. It doesn't matter which ethnic group, race, tribe or nation you are from, Jesus is here. His wellspring of living water is available to you.

Her strength had failed her

She had nowhere to turn

She had no shoulder to cry on

She languished for the life of her son

How could I sit there and watch him die

In this dry deserted place?

A seed of Abraham, could I find grace?

She watched his tears and could do nothing

She did not know someone else was looking

Water in the desert, the word of God is here

I give you living water

Take your fill my dear.

Jesus is the only source of joy and peace

THE PASSOVER LAMB

Exodus 12:1–5 NKJV ...*Every man shall take for himself a lamb, according to the house of his father a lamb for a household.... Your lamb shall be without blemish, a male of the first year.....*

Through Adam's disobedience, every human being sinned and sin reigned in death over the human race, but through Christ's obedience, life has come to all who would believe on His name. The Passover lamb was a shadow of greater things to come. God already had a plan for the salvation of mankind. Jesus has become the Passover lamb. He died the dreadful death of the cross; He was buried, but rose again on the third day. He laid down his life, and He had the power to take it back up again. This act of power is what delivers everyone who believes from the power of darkness. "For God so loved the world that He gave his only begotten son that whosoever believe in him shall not perish but have everlasting life", (John 3:16)

An innocent lamb

Spotless and pure

He waits for the moment

When heaven says its time

The time has come the moment is here

3

The life of one for the sin of many

He laid down His life, without a fight

The Lamb of God, the Father's delight

There is salvation in none other but in Jesus, the only begotten Son of God.

Your Thoughts and Expressions

_____

_____

_____

_____

_____

_____

_____

_____

_____

THE GOD OF GRACE

Exodus 25:21-22 NKJV *"You shall put the mercy seat on top of the ark, and in the ark you shall put the testimony that I give you. And there I will meet with you and speak with you from above the mercy seat…*

The mercy seat, which was placed above the Ark of the Covenant, is symbolic of God's grace. The blood of the sacrificed lamb was sprinkled on it for the atonement of sin. Although the blood of animals was used then, it still required faith for the forgiveness of sins. Today, we have the blood of Jesus which was shed once for all. God will have mercy on whoever comes to that place of atonement to be cleansed by the blood of Jesus. The mercy of God is given to everyone who believes. At the place of atonement, is where the word of God is not challenged. Anyone who has received Jesus as Lord has their hearts cleansed by His blood. What abides now is evidence of the cleansing blood Paul clearly expressed in Ephesians 2:8-9 …*For by grace you have been saved through faith, and that not of yourselves; it is the gift of God, not of works least anyone should boast…*if you have received this gift of grace then no one should condemn you.

Mercy came when I just could not make it

Mercy saw that my strength failed

Mercy said its okay just take it

Mercy atone my case again

"Come let us reason together" says the Lord

Though your sin be as scarlet they shall be as wool

Though they be as crimson

They shall be as white as snow.

Your Thoughts and Expressions

_____

_____

_____

_____

_____

_____

_____

GOD IS ABOVE ALL

Exodus 18:11 NKJV *"Now I know that the Lord is greater than all the gods; for in the very thing in which they behaved proudly. He was above them".*

What was Jethro speaking about? He was speaking about the act of presumption. Pharaoh needed to know in whom all power dwell. He thought he was a power by himself. He figured he was untouchable and unstoppable. God had to let him know who He is. He is God of all creation. The God of the entire universe. Jehovah, God above all. He delivered His people with a mighty hand. The nation of Israel just had to stand still and see the salvation of the Lord.

Sometimes in our walk with God we are faced with challenges. In the midst of all that confronts us, we can forget who is in charge and become confused; quick to confront with harsh words and do things without proper consultation. Stop for a moment and remember who is in charge. He wins all our battles that is why we should let Him fight them. Believers should imitate Christ. Philippians 2:5-11 KJV "Let this mind be in you, which was also in Christ Jesus, Who, being in the form of God, thought it not robbery to be equal with God, But made himself of no reputation, and took upon him the form of a servant, and was made in the likeness of men, And being found in fashion as a man, He humbled himself, and became obedient unto death, even the death of the cross. Wherefore God also hath highly exalted him, and given him a name which is above every name. That at the name of Jesus every knee should bow, of things in heaven, and things in earth, and things under the earth; And that every tongue should confess that Jesus Christ is Lord, to the glory of God the Father. Jesus won the ultimate battle through His humility, and we too can win all our battles if we hold our peace.

Peace be still to every raging tempest

Be at rest ye vehement waves

I speak my word, now ye must obey

I am the Lord who formed you,

I called and ye must hear my voice

Trust in God to win your battles

Your Thoughts and Expressions

_____

_____

_____

"HE IS A MAN OF WAR: THE LORD IS HIS NAME"

Exodus 15:3 NKJV "The Lord is a Man of war; The Lord is His Name".

When Moses declared God as a man of war, he was relishing in the mighty and spectacular victory of Israel. Pharaoh's army was swallowed up by a collapsing wall of water. We are faced with battles everyday of our lives but they are short lived. The war that confronts us is always from the kingdom of darkness. We have a strong tower to run to which is the name of the Lord. When war is raging and the storms are overwhelming all we need to do is to call upon the Lord. He fights our battles and is always victorious. He is our shield and has become our salvation. He is the saving strength of His people. When the battle is won sing your victory song, sing His praise, and exalt His name. The enemy is persistent, but God always has a strategy to overcome him and win the war.

Who are you oh mighty army before Almighty God?

You wrestle all in vain

The words of His mouth shall consume you

A touch of His servant's rod is your demise

Why challenge God Almighty, He has already won the war

Be confident oh child of God

Don't shiver because of the enemy's threat

Just call upon the name of the Lord

He is mighty to save

Father, I thank you for being my rock and fortress. You are my strong tower. Thank you for the victory. In Jesus name. Amen

Your Thoughts and Expressions

_____

_____

_____

_____

_____

_____

_____

HE IS THE WORD OF TRUTH

In Deuteronomy 8:2–3 NKJV *"And you shall remember that the Lord your God led you all the way these forty years in the wilderness, to humble you and test you, to know what's in your heart, whether you would keep His commandments or not. So He humbled you, allowed you to hunger, and fed you with manna which you nor did your fathers know, that man shall not live by bread alone but by every word that proceed from the mouth of the Lord".*

God never speaks an idle word. His word is spirit and life. What He says has power. When we humble ourselves, believe and obey His word, we shall live. Food is for our bodies but the word of God feeds our spirit and abides forever. It is disrespect to God when we let His word fall to the ground and seek to rely on man's philosophy. No matter who that man is, the word of God is greater than any man's wisdom. Ideology and philosophy of men keep men in bondage, but the word of God liberates. Jesus is the word that became flesh, according to John chapter one (1). He said, "I am the way, the truth and the life, no man comes to the father but by me." (John 14:6) Anyone who would have come in contact with Jesus will know that these declarative words are an awesome reality in their life. He whom the Son has set free is free indeed.

Jesus, your word is alive in me. I hunger and thirst for your word each day. Feed me as I read your written word and cause my ear to respond to your spoken word.

Heaven and earth shall pass away, but My words will by no means pass away Mathew 24:35 NKJV

Isaiah 40:8 KJV The grass withereth, the flower fadeth: but the word of our God shall stand for ever.

Your Thoughts and Expressions

_____

_____

_____

_____

_____

_____

_____

_____

_____

_____

HE IS JEHOVAH SHAMMAH

Exodus 20:21 NKJV *"so the people stood far off, but Moses drew near the thick darkness where God was"*

My mind returns to the place where many years ago I can remember when I first heard the voice of God audibly; I was amazed and yet deeply troubled, I felt so unworthy. I was dumfounded, and I froze, but I heard what He said and I knew that it was His voice. It was the purest, most beautiful voice, I've ever heard. The children of Israel may have felt the same way I did, but The Lord's invitation was opened to all who would come to Him. When Moses went up to the mountain, there was a purpose for being there; he needed direction from God to lead His people. God said in 2Corithians 6:16... *"I will dwell in them and walk in them..."* This is how close God wants to get to His people. How closer can He get? He said anyone who comes to me I will in no wise cast out (John 6:37). The awesome presence of God is there for anyone who desires Him. As the Holy Spirit draws you to Christ, you can hear His voice speaking to you also. He desires to speak to you and to lead you into your destiny in Him.

Come up hither

I want to talk to you

To let you know my thoughts of you,

To show you a better way

Come up hither! Draw near

Don't you hear me calling?

Don't be afraid

Shammah, He is ever near

I am present everywhere

Guiding, leading, loving, comforting

Jesus wants you to draw near

Lord, sometimes I feel unworthy to come to you, but I am here. Speak to me Lord; I need to hear from you.

Your Thoughts and Expressions

_____

_____

_____

_____

_____

HE IS GOD OF ALL PEOPLES

Exodus 19:5-6 NKJV *"you shall be to me a kingdom of priests and a Holy nation"*

When God called Israel to be a nation, it was to be separated unto God, so that the gentile nations would be lead to the God of all creation. In Isaiah 42; 6-7, He says "I The Lord, have called you in righteousness; And will hold your hand; I will keep you and give you as a covenant to the people, as a light to the gentiles, to open the blind eyes, to bring out prisoners from the prison, those who sit in darkness from the prison house. I am The Lord that is my name." God's desire is that all people be saved. Israel stumbled but not beyond recovery. They were disobedient so God made salvation available to the gentiles. Now if the gentiles were enriched or empowered because the people of Israel turned down God's offer of salvation, think of how much greater a blessing the world will share when they finally accept it. (Romans 11:72 NLT) All who will come to Jesus shall be a nation of kings and priest. (1Peter 2:9) "But ye are a chosen generation, a royal priest hood, a holy nation, His own special people that you may proclaim the praises of Him who called you out of darkness into His marvelous light".

"But as many as received Him to them gave He power to become the sons of God" (John 1:12 KJV)

I have my father's eyes

And when He cries, I cry

We see the world through the same view

My father's eyes meet mine

I have my father's eyes

When He says go, I go

My hopes and dreams are His

It's my father and me

Your Thoughts and Expressions

_____

_____

_____

_____

_____

_____

_____

HE IS GOD OF YOUR ABUNDANCE

Exodus 20:17 NKJV *…You shall not covet…*

God has increase for all who will seek Him. Jesus said," I have come that they may have life and have it more abundantly…" when we covet others belongings, we hinder our blessings. On the other hand we should be grateful for what we have now and trust God for what He has for us. In Psalms 37:4 the scripture says *"delight yourself in the Lord and He will give you the desires of your heart"*. Today people are so discontented, but God wants our motives to be right. When we walk in a covetous spirit others are hurt; it is destructive, and we are saying to God that what He has for us or given to us is not good enough. Every believer in Christ is guaranteed blessings in this life, but it depends on how much we walk in His counsel.

Always enjoy God's best for you.

I'm counting my blessings

So many they be,

I'm seeking the blesser

He is more than enough for me

Your Thoughts and Expressions

_____

_____

_____

_____

_____

_____

_____

_____

_____

_____

_____

_____

_____

_____

_____

HE IS THE HOLY ANOINTING OIL

Exodus 30:31 NKJV *"And you shall speak to the children of Israel saying, this shall be a holy anointing oil to me throughout your generation".*

In Moses time, the anointing oil was used to consecrate all the things and persons who were dedicated unto service to the Lord. The oil was symbolic of the Holy Ghost. All who have received Jesus into their lives must become driven with a sense of purpose and dedication unto God. The Holy Ghost is poured out into vessels that are separate unto God, hearts that are ready and willing to serve, ready to change their world. He is not given to glorify men, but to give glory to God. In the scripture Moses is warned that the sweet smelling anointing oil should not be used as perfume, nor should anyone try to make an imitation of it. The Holy Ghost is God the Spirit. He is the sweet anointing oil ready to be poured out upon those who earnestly seek Him. When He comes, He empowers, inspires, comforts, and makes your life a sweet smelling savor unto God.

Holy Spirit you are all my heart desire

Touch me, cleanse me, set me on fire

To do the things that pleases my Lord

Grant me strength Father,

To receive your Power and your grace.

Your Thoughts and Expressions

_____

_____

_____

_____

_____

_____

_____

_____

_____

_____

_____

HE IS THE ONE TRUE LIVING GOD

Exodus 23:32-33 NLT *"Make no treaties with them or their gods, they must not live in your land, or they will cause you to sin against me. If you serve their gods you will be caught in a trap of idolatry".*

Jehovah God is not a figment of our imagination. He is real. He is alive. He has no end or any beginning. He is forever. Many people believe this, yet we may still be caught in a trap of idolatry. Idolatry is a snare because it is subtle and does not show itself as it really is. Anything or anyone that is given full devotion, adoration and time, if this is not given to the one true God, is the god we serve. That thing or person is an idol. The trap of idolatry is demonic and will keep you from having a relationship with God who loves us. When we are born again, our spirit desires God more than anything or anyone we find pleasure in. We serve Him not so much for what He can do for us but for whom He is. He is ever present and wants you to know He is there for you. Jesus says, "come onto me, all who labor and are heavy laden and I will give you rest... for my yoke is easy and my burden light". Idolatry puts a yolk upon people and is a heavy, hopeless, bondage, but there is rest in Jesus. Find your rest in Him. (Mathew 11:28-30 NLT)

Love is only found in you

Love is who you are

Let me give my love to you

And not reserve for another

My heart rest in you my God

My heart rest in you

Your Thoughts and Expressions

_____

_____

_____

_____

_____

_____

_____

_____

HE IS THE BREAD OF LIFE

Exodus 16:3-4 NKJV *"Behold I will rain bread from heaven for you..."*

God heard the confession of His people and was ready to feed them with perfectly nutritious food, directly from heaven. The words we speak can chart the course of our destiny. The children of Israel constantly confessed their own death and destruction. They did not believe God. The wise man says, "The eyes of the Lord preserve knowledge, but He overthrows the words of the faithless". (Proverbs 22:12 NKJV) The faithless words were absolutely overthrown by God's miraculous provision of manna from heaven. The true bread of life comes to all who believe. Jesus said to the people *(John 6:29NKJV) "This is the work of God, that you believe in Him whom He sent".* (John 6:32 & 33NKJV)"... Moses did not give you bread from heaven, but my Father gives you the true bread from heaven...for the bread of God is He who comes from heaven and gives life to the world...I am The bread of life."

When all we see is death and destruction, God gives life.

We did not deserve it when He offered Himself

We did not believe but He says here I am

Take my broken body offered for you

Receive my blood which was offered too

Life everlasting is what I give

Take, eat, drink, and live,

Your Thoughts and Expressions

_____

_____

_____

_____

_____

_____

_____

_____

_____

_____

GOD IS OUR PROVIDER

Exodus 25:2 NKJV *"...Speak to the children of Israel that they bring Me an offering. From everyone who gives it willing with his heart you shall take my offering..."*

Giving of offerings is an act of worship. When we give to God, we are saying to Him we are grateful for all that He has provided for us. We are telling Him that we appreciate Him. The offering is not payment to God, it is our gift. The Lord desires offering from a cheerful heart, not grudgingly or stingy, but wholesome and joyful. When our reason for giving is correct, then our gifts would be accepted. The gifts are for the building of the house of the Lord. God does not need our monies or anything from us. When we give, the blessings return to us good measure, pressed down, shaken together and running over; and you will experience increase in your personal life, your home, your communities, and your business, everywhere. Give and do not look back. God knows your heart and is looking at your giving.

Out stretched hands are welcomed,

Where hands are giving,

There are those receiving

A cycle without end.

Keep that cycle rolling

Never stop, my friend

A cheerful heart, a smiling face

And there it goes again.

Your Thoughts and Expressions

_____

_____

_____

_____

_____

_____

_____

_____

_____

HE IS GOD OF THE FIRST FRUIT

Exodus 13:1–2 NKJV *"…Then the Lord spoke to Moses, saying consecrate to me all the first-born, whatever open the womb among the children of Israel both man and beast; it is mine…"*

First, marks beginning. It is a reminder of who God is. He request the first born of both man and beast, and emphasized that it is mine. We often fail to recognize God and place Him First in all things and end up limiting and giving Him, the leftovers. We remember Him when we have trouble or great need. We forget Him when everything is going well, until the trying time comes again. God saved the first born of every household of Israel in Egypt, when the blood of the lamb was placed on the door post. The spirit of death threatened, but the Blood prevailed. God said, "Consecrate to Me the first born "this was a memorial for every household in Israel that the first is significant to Him. He has saved everyone for Himself. When we willingly give our first fruit to God, we are recognizing Him for who He is and are setting the pace for what is to come. It is a seed sown that will bring forth a great harvest.

**BE A GIVER OF FIRST FRUITS,
BE THE REAPER OF GREAT HARVEST**

I am the God of the firsts

I am the first born from the dead

I am the alpha

I am the first born of every creature

I am the one who called light out of darkness

I made the first tree

The first day of the week is mine

I am God of first fruits

Your Thoughts and Expressions

_____

_____

_____

_____

_____

_____

_____

HE IS GOD WHO PRESERVES YOUR WAY

Exodus 16:3 NKJV *"...oh that we had died by the hand of the Lord in Egypt..."*

It is often so easy to look back when faced with challenges. It takes absolutely no big effort. The challenges in life are many, but they are what will push you ahead, if you are focused on your goal. We tend to look back when we forget the distress that was in our lives when we were out there in the world, and had nowhere to turn. We cried out to God and made so many promises and He delivered us. Now we are free, wouldn't it be great to walk in that freedom? Challenges come so that God would prove Himself to you. The fruit of patience is a key element in our Christian growth. James says, "Count it all joy when you fall into various trials knowing that the testing of your faith produces patience". The walk of faith is one of patience. It takes you forward, step by step, never backward. If your eyes are always in the past like Israel in the wilderness, you will just be going around in circles, not finding your way, until you stop to listen and wait for instruction. If you like looking back then let it be for remembering all the great things God has done for you. Be grateful He will surely preserve your way.

TAKE ONE STEP AT A TIME, ONE DAY AT A TIME, AND ONE VICTORY AT A TIME.

Wait! It will be worth it

Wait! Nothing before its time

Every step writes its own chapter

Every moment its lesson to learn.

Your Thoughts and Expressions

_____

_____

_____

_____

_____

_____

_____

_____

_____

_____

GOD IS MORE THAN ENOUGH

Exodus 16:12, 13 NKJV *"...I have heard the complaints of the children of Israel. Speak to them, saying, At twilight you shall eat meat and in the evening you shall be filled with bread. And you shall know I am the Lord your God."*

Sometimes we are not able to see God for who He really is. We doubt and complain. We are not satisfied. That is when God shows Himself to be the God who is more than enough. He ensures that we are satisfied. Even though complaining may not be the right approach God still responds. God wants us to be happy and enjoy our lives every day in Him. Jesus says, *"I have come that you may have life and have it more abundantly"*. God did not just want to give an abundance of food to His people. He wanted them to know who He is. He does not lack anything. He is our all sufficiency. He does not delay in delivering but comes through at the right time. We all need to be comforted in God's love rather than complaining. Rest in His abundance.

El shaddai, you are all I need

You fill my heart's desire

You rain blessings on me every day

Thank you, thank you,

Almighty God you are more than enough You are my Lord indeed.

Your Thoughts and Expressions

_____

_____

_____

_____

_____

_____

_____

_____

_____

_____

_____

HE IS OUR INTERCESSOR

Exodus 32:11 NKJV *"...Then Moses pleaded with the Lord his God and said: "Lord why does your wrath burn hot against your people...?"*

The intercessor is one who is selfless. We need their prayer when the storms of life are up against us. We need them when we are blind, stubborn, rebellious, backslidden. Their prayer is what will bring us back on the right track. The intercessor is not self righteous, but considers the righteousness of God. They consider others and remember God's promises, His feats, and His name. Moses stood in the gap for the people of God, when God was ready to destroy them and make a nation for Himself out of Moses. God was filled with righteous indignation, so Moses had to plead with Him, to spare the people whom He had recently delivered with a mighty hand. Today we have an intercessor in the persons of Jesus Christ and The Holy Ghost whom He sent. He is constantly standing in the gap for us, so that we may obtain His promises.

Hebrews 7:25 NKJV... *"Therefore He is also able to save to the uttermost those who come to God through Him, since He always lives to make intercession for them..."*

I plead your cause

I present your case

Your advocate watching for you

Your heavenly Father assures your destiny

Keep looking ahead

Jesus intercedes for you

Your Thoughts and Expressions

_____

_____

_____

_____

_____

_____

_____

_____

HE IS GOD WHO HEALS

Exodus 15:26 NKJV *"…For I am the Lord who heals you…"*

Our health is usually an area of great challenge in our lives. When sickness comes, we sometimes worry, and spend a lot of money, because we want the best solution. The Lord said," I am the Lord who heals you". Can God heal you? Of course He can. Only believe that all things are possible with God. Jesus was chastised for our healing. He bore the stripes on His body for us. He said to the lame man at the troubled water, John 5:5-9, KJV "wilt thou be made whole"? Immediately he was healed. Jesus is not just our Savior, He is our healer. If sickness shows up at anytime in your life, be affirmed that God gave His word, "I am the Lord who heals you".

The healer is in your house

The deliverer is in this temple

If only you trust Him you will be whole

This temple in which He dwell

Made pure for His residing

Your Thoughts and Expressions

HE DEFENDS THE FAITHFUL

Numbers 12:6-8 NKJV "*...Then He said, hear now my words; if there is a prophet among you, I the Lord make myself known to him in a vision. I speak to him in a dream. Not so with my servant Moses. He is faithful in all my house. I speak to him face to face. Even plainly and not in dark sayings...*"

Often, believers find themselves back biting their Pastors and leaders. They utter words that will discredit them and tarnish their integrity. In doing this, they are seeking personal gain and encouraging strife. We must always know that God gives us faithful leaders who watch for us, and He watches for them. He would not sit back and let fiery darts be hurled at His servants and not defend them. He made an example of Miriam, when He struck her with leprosy and gave her time to repent. Moses interceded for her and she was healed. God is listening to your conversation and you inner gripes. Take heed less you find yourself in a similar position as Miriam. Pray for leaders and those God has placed over you. The decisions they make are not their own. The words they speak are not their own. They are not their own.

Listen to your leaders,

Pay attention to their cry,

Just listen for a moment.

The words they speak is from God on high

Pray that they continue to walk with God each day

Respect and love your leaders.

They are watching for you today.

Your Thoughts and Expressions

_____

_____

_____

_____

_____

_____

_____

_____

_____

HE IS LORD IN THE MIDST OF THE TABERNACLE

Exodus 40:34-38 NKJV *"...Then the cloud covered the tabernacle of meeting, and the glory of the Lord filled the tabernacle..."*

It is amazing how the glory of the Lord was manifest among His people. The Lord's presence gave assurance to them and comfort. A pillar of cloud by day and a fire by night. When the glory of the Lord moved from the tabernacle, it was time to move. God literally dwelt with His people and walked with them. Never at any time should they feel abandoned or rejected. Today, His seal is on HIS saints. Yes, born again believers are marked with His seal. **Ephesians 1:13,14 NJKV** "In Him you also trusted after you heard the word of truth, the gospel of your salvation; in whom also having believed, you were sealed with the Holy Spirit of Promise who is the guarantee of our inheritance... to the praise of His glory". The presence of God in His people guarantees their inheritance in Christ.

Bless every moment we gather Lord

Let your presence be manifest

Let the fruit of our lips bring you praise

Let our ears be ready to hear your command

Let our spirits be discerning to know your leading

Let our hearts understand the time in which we live

Your Thoughts and Expressions

_____

_____

_____

_____

_____

_____

_____

_____

_____

_____

THE LORD IS MY BANNER (JEHOVAH NISSI)

Exodus 17:8-16 NKJV vs 12 "…so Aaron and Hur supported his hands, one on one side and the other on the other side ; and his hands were steady until the going down of the sun…"

Who is holding up your hands?

Sometimes when we are in leadership, the journey can be heavy and very burdensome. Your hands may grow weak, feeble and feel even tied up. The battle rages on. In the scriptures we see that Moses, the servant of the Lord, in the midst of battle was not left alone. He had two great helpers standing on either side of him holding up his hands. This was the key to their victory over their enemy, the Amalekites. They saw the need and seized the opportunity, not to enter into battle by taking the sword but by letting him sit down and holding up his hands. God has become their Jehovah Nissi, their mighty banner. Likewise in church life today, we should also seize the opportunity to be a source of added strength and help to those in leadership; make their work less burdensome and encourage them, letting them know they can count on you. They are not meant to walk alone. The banner of God is lifted high when we work together. Victory is ahead.

STOP! LOOK! HELP IS HERE.

Faithful is he who is a friend

Take the charge to hold a hand

Walk the distance, walk with you

Striding close to see you through

He lifts His banner. He is JEHOVAH NISSI

Your Thoughts and Expressions

_____

_____

_____

_____

_____

_____

_____

_____

_____

HE IS OUR COUNSELLOR

Exodus 18:13-24 NKJV vs 19 *"...Listen to my voice; I will give you counsel and God will be with you..."*

The voice of counsel is never a voice of confusion. It puts in order what is in disarray and turmoil. The counsel of the Lord is in the voice of others who are concerned about you and are seeking your best interest." Plans go wrong for the lack of advice; many advisors bring success" (**Proverbs 15:22 NLT**) It was truly tiring what Moses was doing. The counsel of his father-in- law made easier the task he had. Jethro was a remarkable administrator. Moses welcomed his counsel passionately. God brought him to the camp just at the right time. His presence was like a breath of fresh air. When he left, Moses had already implemented the plan. Our attitude to counsel matters more than the counsel itself. Accept good counsel, it may just be what will bring your break through.

Searching, wondering, seeking

Tired, how can I get through this all on my own?

A wind of change came blowing

My eyes were opened, I see the light

Now who are you oh great mountain

Just one word of wisdom and you are no more in sight

My eyes are opened, I see the way

The voice of true counsel made my day

Your Thoughts and Expressions

_____

_____

_____

_____

_____

_____

_____

_____

_____

_____

THE LORD WHO SETS US APART

Exodus 19:14 NKJV *"And Moses went down from the mountain to the people and sanctified the people and they washed their clothes…"*

When I think of sanctification, I think of Paul's instructions to Timothy in 2 Tim 2:20 that in a great house there are not only vessels of gold and of silver, but there are different vessels laid aside for the masters use. Every vessel is different and has a special purpose. Have you ever thought of your value to the master? We have been washed by the blood of Jesus and are sanctified unto Him. Moses was instructed by the Lord to sanctify the people. He has set them apart to be His own special treasure, but He required them to be obedient to His commands and to be a holy people. They willingly received the words of Moses, washed themselves, and was ready to meet with God. Then, the power and majesty of God was so great, they could not bear it but the scripture says to us who are His people today in **Hebrews 12:22 NKJV,** "…but you have come to mount Zion, the city of the living God, the heavenly Jerusalem, to an innumerable company of angels". Having this assurance we can approach God's throne with great confidence. Knowing that we are set apart and washed in the blood of Jesus, gives us confidence to be effective in service to Him, because our lives are pure and holy unto Him.

He holds in his hands a vessel

Perfectly carved for His own use

He gently pours in oil mixed with sweet perfume

A vessel of honor made for His own use

He takes the vessel through every path He leads

His light shine through this vessel

That brightens every dark corner of the world

Your Thoughts and Expressions

_____

_____

_____

_____

_____

_____

_____

_____

THE LORD WHO KEEPS

Exodus 6:4 KJV *"…I have also established my covenant with them, the land of their pilgrimage where in they were strangers…"*

There are times in life when we question whether we will make it to the end. These thoughts usually haunt us and lead us to want to quit; to give up on our marriage, to go cold in our relationships, to lay aside the things we love and enjoy in life. A young wife worried one day if her marriage would last. She wondered if her husband's affection is for her or some other woman. She started thinking maybe we should end this marriage right now, before there is any hurt. So she decided in her mind what she wants for herself or what the husband will have. Cautiously being lead down a road to destruction of another family. Then the Lord intervene by saying," I am the Lord who keeps". He often reminds us that He keeps His promises to us and whatever we commit to Him He will keep. **2Timothy 1:12 NKJV** Paul says to Timothy "…I know whom I believe and I am persuaded that He is able to keep what I have committed to Him until that day…"

The enemy is a thief. He will steal from us if we allow him to. We must remain fixed on the word of God. He is not only able to keep His promises, but He also keeps what we commit to Him.

Where my knees are feeble,

He strengthens

Where my heart quivers

He comforts

When my spirit is broken,

He mends

When my mind is weak, He gives His word

He is the Lord who keeps, Jehovah is His name.

Your Thoughts and Expressions

_____

_____

_____

_____

_____

_____

HE CLOTHES YOU IN HIS RIGHTEOUSNESS

Exodus 28:2 NKJV *"...And you shall make Holy garments for Aaron your brother, for glory and for beauty..."*

The day I received Jesus as my Lord I actually felt the newness. It was like brand new clothing was placed on my inner being and a load was lifted off me. The burden of sin was no more on me. I was now clothed in the righteousness of Christ. I was only twelve years old and deep down in my heart I knew I found a real treasure that I would hold on to for the rest of my life. This treasure is one that I can share with others, not hold on to for myself.

The priestly garment was a true beauty; all those precious stones, the brilliant colors, are a genuine reflection of Christ our Lord, who holds His people so close to His heart. He clothed me with an outstanding garment to reflect His beauty and His glory. What an awesome God He is! **Psalms 132:9 KJV** says," Let your priest be clothed with righteousness and let your saints shout for joy." He gives us reasons to shout. In **Isaiah 64:6 NKJV** says "... all our righteousnesses are like filthy rags..." When we are born again, He clothed us in His righteousness, to shine His light in this dark world.

Filthy rags blowing in the wind

Torn and tattered

Waving vigorously saying goodbye

Thrown away forever

Brand new garment fit for royalty

Flowing, glowing, going on a journey new

Your Thoughts and Expressions

_____

_____

_____

_____

_____

_____

_____

_____

_____

HE IS THE GOD OF TRUTH

Exodus 20:16 KJV *"...Thou shall not bear false witness against thy neighbor..."*

There are people who are gifted in damaging the image of others: They would outfit another in a character that does not fit them and make a monster of them. When we open our mouths to speak of someone, we must make sure it is the truth and it is for the right reason. Sometimes in talking we may have envy, hatred, unforgiveness, and resentment in our hearts, so instead of speaking in love, we speak in those spirits. That is misrepresenting someone and bearing false witness. It is just like lying in court under oath.

We are made in the image of God and should bear Godly character once we are born again. Jesus says, "I am the way, the truth and the life..." If the spirit of truth lives in us, then let us walk in the truth and speak truth about each other, building up one another, speaking encouraging words.

When the Lord commanded, do not bear false witness against thy neighbor, He is encouraging us to speak the truth about others. **In Proverbs 6:19 KJV** among the seven things God hates is a false witness that speaks lies. Satan is the father of lies. We are not his children. Let us speak the truth of each other and walk as children of light.

I hear a voice the brings me peace

I have nothing to hide from Him

I am exposed before Him and yet He hides me

Deep in His secret place

I hear a voice that brings me comfort

There alone I find my rest.

The rest truth brings

Because His truth has made me free.

Your Thoughts and Expressions

_____

_____

_____

_____

_____

_____

_____

HE IS THE LORD WHO RESTORES

Jeremiah 30:17 NKJV "...*For I will restore health to you and heal you of your wounds, says the Lord...*"

Sometimes the beating that life gives is so severe, it leaves us with it wounds that are painful and constantly oozing. They can be wounds inflicted by persons close to you, or the consequences we face because of our own foolish decisions. Constant reminders of these evils are like solemn songs of mourning. They just make you sad and cause your heart to sink in a deep sorrowful grave.

Should all our days be filled with misery?

God truly is our refuge and strength, a very present help in times of trouble. He comes to us in our wounded state and gives us the word of His assurance. He assures health, which is, wholesomeness within and without. What is better than peace of mind? Thank God, He never walk's pass a wounded heart. He offers an outstretched hand to those who are wounded and gives them a reason to smile again.

Be sure to grab hold of His healing hand.

Smile, yes Jesus can put the sparkle back in your smile

Laugh out loud and crackle let the whole world know

You are back on the stage of life to play your part in full

Give it your best shot, the bygones are gone and you are on your way

Marking your stride every day. Standing strong and standing tall

I know God still love me after all.

Your Thoughts and Expressions

_____

_____

_____

_____

_____

_____

_____

HE IS THE BRONZE SERPENT

Numbers 21:8 NKJV *"…Then the Lord said to Moses, Make a fiery serpent and set it on a pole; and it shall be, that everyone who is bitten, when he looks at it, shall live…"*

Jesus said to Nicodemus (**John 3:14–15 NKJV**)… "As Moses lifted up the serpent in the wilderness, even so must the Son of Man be lifted up, that whosoever believes in Him shall not perish but have eternal life…". The bronze serpent was the focal point for anyone who was bitten by the fiery serpent after Israel sinned in the wilderness, if they wanted to live. It is the same way Jesus Christ is the focal point for anyone who wants to be saved. He will deliver your soul from eternal death and Hell. He is the ONLY source of eternal life. The walk of faith is a life of steadfastness. We cannot walk except we keep our eyes on Him. We are saved when we centre our focus on Him. The moment we take our eyes off Him, we begin to sink; we become trapped in our own world or someone else's. Soon thereafter, doubt and unbelief steps in, that will take us down a road to death. The people in the wilderness realized that their only hope to live was to look to the bronze serpent. Let us who live now, never lose sight of Christ our Savior who was lifted up for us.

Tracing His steps like a toddler in her mother's shoes

Hoping one day to be just like Him

Embracing every word He says

Loving every moment with Him

Trusting in His loving care

Your Thoughts and Expressions

_____

_____

_____

_____

_____

_____

_____

_____

_____

HE IS LORD OF THE SABBATH

Exodus 20:11 KJV "*Wherefore the Lord blessed the Sabbath day and hallowed it….*"

The Sabbath day has become controversial, but that was never God's intention. He is not the author of confusion. It was hallowed and blessed, but the understanding of Sabbath is simply rest. God rested on the Sabbath day. He took the time to enjoy the beauty of His excellent work of creation. Sabbath gracefully explains what should be done after a great job was completed. After God made everything, He said it was good, and then He rested. This does not mean He went to sleep. He is still creating and bringing to life all who are dead in trespasses and sin.

After being accused of working on the Sabbath day, Jesus said to His accusers," the Sabbath was made for man, and not man for the Sabbath, therefore the son of man is Lord of the Sabbath" **(Mark 2:27–28 KJV).** He was there in the beginning before the Sabbath was established. The Sabbath was not a burden placed on man, but was a time-off for man to stop, be grateful, recuperate, and get back to work. It does not mean that a kind deed should not be done, or lives should not be saved. It was given in love, so it should be received with love.

Stop. Rest for a while

Watch the garden blossom

See the fruit trees grow

Look at the potential of every seed

Just a small life in the earth

The wheel of life abounds, more and more.

Your Thoughts and Expressions

_____

_____

_____

_____

_____

_____

_____

_____

THE ROD OF DELIVERANCE

EXODUS 4:20 KJV *"…and Moses took the rod of God in his hand…"*

The rod of the shepherd has become the rod of God, a tool in Moses hand to demonstrate the power of God. Moses was commissioned to lead God's people out of bondage just like the shepherd leads his flock. This rod became his mark of authority and a tool of deliverance. Jesus was referred to as the rod out of the stem of Jesse. He has given authority to all who will believe and trust in Him. He commissioned His disciples saying, "…go into all the world and preach the gospel to every creature…" (**Mathew 28:19 KJV**). Now, the rod is placed in every believer's hand. Jesus said to His disciples, "these signs shall follow them that believe, they shall heal the sick, cast out demons…." (**Mark 16:17 KJV**). The rod is a reminder for us to know that we have the authority to lead men out of bondage. Like Moses, God has commissioned us to carry the rod of deliverance. Let us take it and use it.

We hold the rod of deliverance in our hand

With the gospel of peace our feet is shod

Breaking walls in the name of the Lord

Setting up His banner territories mark

Proclaiming His name and not turning back.

Your Thoughts and Expressions

_____

_____

_____

_____

_____

_____

_____

_____

_____

_____

_____

_____

THE LORD OF OUR SUNSET

Deuteronomy 33:1 KJV *And this is the blessings where with Moses the man of God blessed the children of Israel before his death....*

The closing days of man on earth are known to him. The Lord would not keep it a secret. We cannot get away from the fact that one day the Lord will take the hand of His saints and walk away with them into eternity. Moses made full use of his life doing God's will. He did not walk away without leaving a blessing with God's people. He reminded them of the faithfulness of God from the time he met Him at Sinai to the present where the children of Israel were about to enter the Promised Land and His promise was about to be fulfilled. There was no complaining with Moses, God said it was time to go and he was ready. The fulfillment of his days on earth has ended and he was now entering a new and even more exiting life with The Lord.

We must be reminded of an even greater promise of being with the Lord in heaven also. The scripture says "...we are confident, yes, well pleased rather to be absent from the body and to be present with the Lord..." (**2 Corinthians 5:8 NKJV**.)

Moses confidently gave his last words to the people of God..." Happy are you O Israel! Who is like you, a people saved by the Lord? The shield of your help and the sword of your majesty! Your enemies shall submit to you, and you shall tread down their high places…"

The Lord walks him to mount Nebo and showed him all the land of Israel, then He walked with him to glory.

It is never too late when God says it is time

To stride to the rhythm of His voice

Marching onward to eternity

Lifting high His banner

Stamping His authority on earth.

Your Thoughts and Expressions

_____

_____

_____

_____

_____

_____

HE QUENCHES OUR THIRST

Exodus 17:1-7 NKJV vs. 6 *"Behold, I will stand before you there on the rock in Horeb; and you shall strike the rock, and water will come out of it, that the people may drink." And Moses did so in the sight of the elders of Israel".*

When water runs out, it is a tragedy. This precious life giving substance is expected to always be in abundance. We only miss water when thirst sets in and our tongues claves to the roof of our mouths, and the throat is parched and dry. The quest for water became a great challenge for Israel in the wilderness but Israel did not believe it was their duty to go looking for water. They clamored with Moses angrily and were about to stone him. This caused him to cry out to God.

We may sometimes grow dry in our spiritual life, and feel like the well spring of life in Christ has dried up. What do we do then? Blame our Pastors and leaders, or do we look to the source of our joy? It is imperative as believers that we take responsibility for our Christian life. Tiny baby birds are fed mouth to mouth by their parents, but as they grow older they go out and find their own food. These simple lessons in nature should show us that, with God, all that we need is available to us but we should seek Him for it. (**Psalms 42:1-2NKJV**)"... As the deer pants for the water brooks so pants my soul for you, o God. My soul thirsts for God, for the living God..."

There is a greater thirst

There is a longing deep within the soul

Strike the rock of your salvation

The head corner stone

He is the Lord that never fails.

Your Thoughts and Expressions

_____

_____

_____

_____

_____

_____

_____

_____

_____

HE IS THE FATHER OF JESHURUN

Deuteronomy 33:26 NKJV *"There is no God like the God of Jeshurun, who rides the heavens to help you"*

When fathers call their children by a pet name, it stirs up joy and put a spark in the relationship. It will cause that child to want to be close to their father every day. When children know they are loved, the relationship between them and their parents will grow stronger. It will not be lopsided; it is not just about taking, but giving. The Lord called Israel by that special name Jeshurun, which means *"upright one"*. This was His purpose for His people.

In the closing chapter of Malachi, he prophesied "…to you who fear my name, the Sun of righteousness shall appear with healing in His wings…He will turn the heart of the fathers to the children and the heart of the children to the fathers…" (**Malachi 4:2&6 NKJV**). This statement revealed that father's relationship with their children can become strained, but there is a binding factor who is Jesus Christ, the Son of righteousness. He knows the heart of His father and through Him, we can return to our heavenly Father. He gives a new name to all His children. **Revelation 3:12 NKJV**…And I will write on him my new name… God has that special name He calls you by, that name no one knows, but only he who receives it, **Revelation 2:17 NKJV**. That name is pointing you towards your destiny in Him; let this be your delight and greatest desire as you draw nearer to God. He will draw near to you. (James 5:7-8)

God of Jeshurun, your name is excellent

God of our fathers you are precious to me

You carry me on eagle's wings and hide me in your secret place

You feed me until I am satisfied

You make me your own

I am the apple of your eye

Your Thoughts and Expressions

_____

_____

_____

_____

_____

_____

OUR GOD IS HOLY

Exodus 28:36 NKJV *"You shall also make a plate of pure gold and engrave on it, like the engraving of a signet: HOLINESS TO THE LORD.*

Godly character reflects the image of God in every human being, who is truly born again by His Holy Spirit. The new birth is a change of heart that is initiated and sustained by the Holy Spirit. The Lord said, And you shall be Holy; for I am Holy… (**Leviticus 11:44 NKJV**) In the New Testament Peter added (**1Peter 1:15–16**) As He who has called you is Holy, you also be Holy in your conduct… He emphasizes that we are not bought with corruptible things but with the precious blood of Jesus as a lamb without blemish or spot. Jesus walk this earth with unquestionable character. Pilate testified that he found no fault in Him. Jesus walked with purpose and sought to do the will of His father. This is true Holiness. Our conviction, love and desire to please God will help us to walk in the Spirit and not in condemnation. "Walk in the Spirit and you will not fulfill the lust of the flesh" (Galatians5:16 NKJV). God by His Spirit will lead us to a life of holiness, a reflection of the image of God; a life sold out to Christ and His will.

God order my steps in your word

Humble my heart

Preserve my way

Let me be a true reflection of your image

Your Thoughts and Expressions

_____

_____

_____

_____

_____

_____

_____

_____

_____

HE IS OUR SANCTUARY

Exodus 15:17 KJV ...*Thou shalt bring them in and plant them in the mountain of thine inheritance, in the place O Lord for you to dwell, in the sanctuary which thine hands have established...*

The song of Moses rehearsed the Lord's promise to His people which was already established by His word. It was already established in Israel that the Lord was with them. As every establishment has its foundation laid by its leaders, the foundation was laid down for the church by the Lord. God lead the people of Israel and established them upon the rock of His authority and planted them upon the foundation of His word.

Jesus asked His disciples one day, who do men, say I am? Then He asked who do you say I am? The revelation came to Peter and he answered, you are the Christ, the Son of the living God. Jesus fervently responded ... you are Peter, and upon this rock I will build my church... **(Mathew 16:13–16)** The solid rock is Christ, the only begotten Son of God; the sanctuary in which men can find refuge, the truth that stands and makes men free.

Lord I found you to be a sanctuary

A holy place to dwell

You have brought me in and out in safety

And that my soul knows so well

Your Thoughts and Expressions

_____

_____

_____

_____

_____

_____

_____

_____

_____

_____

HE ENSURES YOUR INHERITANCE

Numbers 27:1–8 KJV ...*Thou shalt surely give them a possession of an inheritance among their father's brethren*....

Asking for what you want is what the Lord desires. Jesus said in John 16:24, "Until now you have not ask for anything in my name".

The daughters of Zelophehad knew what it means to ask. Their father died at the judgment of Korah but they did not let it be to their condemnation. They knew their rights as children of God, a chosen people. They knew they had a place in Israel. Asking can be hard for some of us especially when we seem to be under a cloud of condemnation, or even when we are afraid of being denied. Yes, God knows what is in our hearts, but we need to verbalize it. Expressing your desire is what God wants. He is not short on anything; He is willing to give you what is rightfully yours and would put all measures in place to ensure you have it. There is an inheritance in God's kingdom for all who believes. Seek Him and you will definitely find what abundance is available to you.

Let my asking be simple

Exactly what I want, I ask

I know who I ask has more

Let me ask without wavering

For I know there will be nothing from you for me

If I am like a ship without a rudder, tossed about the sea

Your Thoughts and Expressions

_____

_____

_____

_____

_____

_____

_____

_____

HE IS GOD OF EVERY GENERATION

Numbers 27:16-18 KJV ....let the LORD, the God of the Spirit of all flesh, set a man over the congregation.....

Taking the next generation forward requires fortitude, courage and a disciplined leader. Moses knew this very well. The question before him was who will God have to lead His people? It was not His biding to put a man in that place. It was the Lord's. There was no need for political campaign. God knew exactly who He wanted to lead His people. Joshua was the understudy of Moses, yet he did not give any suggestion, but left it to God to choose who He wanted.

The charge of shepherd and warrior was placed on Joshua. He had to take the land the Lord has given His people. Moses lead Israel out of Egypt, now forty years later, Joshua is leading them into the Promised Land. Providing leadership to possess the land required character and relationship. These are important to God. If a man does not have a relationship with God heart to heart, how would He follow God's direction?

The charge laid on Christ was hard, but He willingly took it. The scripture says, it pleased the father to bruise Him.... Yet His desire was to please the Father. How about you? God may just place a charge on you to take a city, a nation or the family next door. The Lord promised Joshua He will be with him, just as He was with Moses.

He will also be with you, if you accept His charge. Jesus, the high priest will defiantly lay His hand on you, anoint you and accompany you into battle.

Lord, I have nothing in my hand not even a rod

But what you give to me I'll take it

I'll go if you say go, but all I ask is that you go before me

Your Thoughts and Expressions

_____

_____

_____

_____

_____

_____

_____

_____

I AM THAT I AM

Exodus 3:14 KJV And God said to Moses, I am that I am: and He said, thus shall thou say unto the children of Israel, I AM hath sent me unto you...

I AM. What an amazing name! The feeling that comes with that name gives such assurance. I AM means always present, anything and everything, you will ever need. The name I AM will not be a mystery to anyone who knows the Almighty God. Knowing I AM brings peace and comfort to all who search for Him. Israel in Egypt must have felt as time went by that the God of their fathers had forgotten them. They were crying out in, and from their affliction in Egypt. The Lord, I AM, heard and came to give them hope.

The Sinai experience became a lifelong walk with I AM, with many lessons to be thought throughout the ages, climaxing with the gift of God, the Lord, the Messiah, the Christ, Jesus our savior. What was meant to be a three day journey became forty years in the wilderness, yet I AM never left them. He was always present. Always. Every moment gave them more reasons to trust Him. In every battle they faced His standard was raised. The shackles of this world are overwhelming, but Jesus has overcome the world. He said... "I AM the door: by me if any man enters in, he shall be saved and shall go in and out and find pasture..." (**John 10:9 KJV**). His name, I

AM is an invitation to you that He is here to fulfill your every need. Let Him be Lord of your life.

He offers eternal life. (**John 17:3 KJV**)... and this is eternal life, that they might know thee, the only true God, and Jesus Christ, whom thou hast sent...

I AM. You bring hope to me

Never thought I would make it

You are always by my side

I AM. You make me complete

Like a master builder you put all my broken pieces together

I am forever grateful, that day you held my hand and walked with me

You are my forever friend.

Your Thoughts and Expressions

_____

_____

_____

WORKS CITED

Printed Bibles

Authorised King James Version Bible. World Bible
Publishers Inc, 2000.

The New King James Version, Topical Reference Edition;
Thomas Nelson Inc., 1994.

Life Application Study Bible. New Living Translation,
2nd Edition. Tyndale House Publishers Inc., 2007